p e a r l s

o f   w i s d o m

Heaven: It's a Party and You're Invited

Shirley Perich

krēgel
PUBLICATIONS

Grand Rapids, MI 49501

Pearls of Wisdom: Heaven: It's a Party and You're Invited

© 2002 by Shirley Perich

Published by Kregel Publications, a division of Kregel, Inc., P.O. Box 2607, Grand Rapids, MI 49501. For more information about Kregel Publications, visit our Web site: www.kregel.com.

Scripture quotations marked NIV are from the *Holy Bible, New International Version.* © 1973, 1978, 1984 by International Bible Society. Used by permission of Zondervan Publishing House. All rights reserved.

Scripture quotations marked NLT are from the *Holy Bible,* New Living Translation, © 1996. Used by permission of Tyndale House Publishers, Inc., Wheaton, Illinois 60189. All rights reserved.

Scripture quotations marked NCV are from *The Holy Bible, New Century Version.* © 1987, 1988, 1991 by Word Publishing, Dallas, Texas 75234. Used by permission.

ISBN 0-8254-3561-7

Printed in the United States of America

1 2 3 / 06 05 04 03 02

pearls

of wisdom

No eye has seen,
no ear has heard,
and no mind has
imagined what God has
prepared for those who
love him.

1 Corinthians 2:9
(NLT)

It's a party and
you're invited!

For: You
Date: Today
Place: Wherever you are

"Now go out to the street corners and invite everyone you see." So the servants brought in everyone they could find, good and bad alike, and the banquet hall was filled with guests.

Matthew 22:9-10
(NLT)

No chance this invitation's getting lost in the mail. It comes special delivery.

"Look! Here I stand at the door and knock. If you hear me calling and open the door, I will come in, and we will share a meal as friends."

Revelation 3:20
(NLT)

This party's in a neighborhood that'll knock your socks off.

The twelve gates were made of pearls—each gate from a single pearl! And the main street was pure gold, as clear as glass.

Revelation 21:21
(NLT)

And you simply don't have
a thing to wear?
No problem.

The Lord makes me very happy. . . . He has covered me with clothes of salvation and wrapped me with a coat of goodness, like a bridegroom dressed for his wedding.

Isaiah 61:10
(NCV)

No need to bother with your minks, diamonds, or Cadillacs. They wouldn't impress anyone at this party anyway.

After all, we didn't bring anything with us when we came into the world, and we certainly cannot carry anything with us when we die.

1 Timothy 6:7
(NLT)

Come hungry.
You can pretty much
count on it being a
catered affair.

You feed them
from the abundance of
your own house, let-
ting them drink from
your rivers
of delight.

Psalm 36:8
(NLT)

A new version of you is a standard party gift (and we're not talking your average Hollywood makeover here).

We grow weary in our present bodies, and we long for the day when we will put on our heavenly bodies like new clothing.

2 Corinthians 5:2
(NLT)

Door prizes, too.

(Well, actually, prizes with doors.)

"There are many rooms in my Father's home, and I am going to prepare a place for you. If this were not so, I would tell you plainly."

John 14:2
(NLT)

Not to mention party bags
filled with crowns
and stars.

"To all who are victorious, who obey me to the very end, I will give authority over all the nations. They will have the same authority I received from my Father, and I will also give them the morning star!"

Revelation 2:26, 28
(NLT)

Oh, there is one catch
(doggone that fine print).
You have to be perfect
to attend.

"But you are to be
perfect, even as your
Father in heaven
is perfect."

Matthew 5:48
(NLT)

About now, are you think-
ing you could have saved
somebody a lot of trouble?
You never claimed to be
perfect so whose invita-
tion did
you get by mistake?

The Lord says, "Come,
let us talk about these
things. Though your
sins are like scarlet,
they can be as
white as snow."

Isaiah 1:18
(NCV)

Can you believe God
looks at you and sees
a halo?

Yeah, that's right—you.

He declared us not
guilty because of his
great kindness.

Titus 3:7
(NLT)

That's because He's paid for every single dumb, selfish, thoughtless, unkind, greedy, knuckle-headed, opinionated, self-righteous...

OK. OK. We get the picture. Point is, it's all forgiven.

He forgave all our sins. He canceled the debt, which listed all the rules we failed to follow. He took away that record with its rules and nailed it to the cross.

Colossians 2:13–14
(NCV)

Yup.
Paid for.
In full.

He is so rich in kindness that he purchased our freedom through the blood of his Son, and our sins are forgiven.

Ephesians 1:7
(NLT)

Gone.
Really gone.

He has taken
our sins away from
us as far as the
east is from west.

Psalm 103:12
(NCV)

And forgotten.

(So don't go reminding Him—He won't know what you're talking about.)

"I, I am the One who
forgives all your sins,
for my sake;
I will not remember
your sins."

Isaiah 43:25
(NCV)

For free.
Really.

Not gonna find a string
attached to this one.

We have forgiveness of sins. How rich is God's grace, which he has given to us so fully and freely.

Ephesians 1:7–8
(NCV)

Not an easy concept for those of us living in a world where nothing is free—outside of maybe a few samples at the grocery store on Saturday.

God gives us a free
gift—life forever
in Christ Jesus
our Lord.

Romans 6:23
(NCV)

That's a pretty good deal
for those of us who act like
cheese balls now
and again.

Thank God for
his Son—a gift
too wonderful
for words!

2 Corinthians 9:15
(NLT)

It's enough to make you want to throw a party yourself, isn't it?

"Oh, what joy for those whose disobedience is forgiven, whose sins are put out of sight.

Yes, what joy for those whose sin is no longer counted against them by the Lord."

Romans 4:7–8
(NLT)

Rest assured. It was not a computer error that landed your name on this guest list.

I have called you
by name, and you
are mine.

Isaiah 43:1
(NCV)

Being good has nothing to do with being invited.

If that were the case we'd all have to RSVP with regrets.

Salvation is not a reward for the good things we have done, so none of us can boast about it.

Ephesians 2:9
(NLT)

If you're still wondering why He so badly wants you to come, well, He enjoys your company.

The LORD's
delight is in those who
honor him, those who
put their hope in his
unfailing love.

Psalm 147:11
(NLT)

And He loves you.

You are God's children
whom he loves.

Ephesians 5:1
(NCV)

And not just a little.

Christ's love is greater than anyone can ever know.

Ephesians 3:19
(NCV)

In fact, a whole,
whole lot.

May you have
the power to under-
stand, as
all God's people
should, how wide, how
long, how high, and
how deep his love real-
ly is.

Ephesians 3:18
(NLT)

Don't believe 'em
when they tell you death
and taxes are
the only things you
can count on.

"The mountains may disappear, and the hills may come to an end, but my love will never disappear; my promise of peace will not come to an end," says the LORD who shows mercy to you.

Isaiah 54:10
(NCV)

So, in the midst of
all this love, why is there
pain, illness,
and death?

"Here on earth you
will have many trials
and sorrows.
But take heart,
because I have over-
come the world."

John 16:33
(NLT)

Fact is, we simply aren't promised a rose garden this side of heaven. (We blew that concept pretty early on with a piece of fruit.)

For our present troubles are quite small and won't last very long. Yet they produce for us an immeasurably great glory that will last forever!

2 Corinthians 4:17
(NLT)

Everybody has troubles,
because we all have les-
sons to learn.

Even though Jesus
was the Son of
God, he learned obedi-
ence by what he suf-
fered. And because his
obedience was perfect,
he was able to give
eternal salvation to all
who obey him.

Hebrews 5:8–9
(NCV)

That makes the ride
to the party a little
rough sometimes.
In fact, sometimes
it's downright bumpy.
And sometimes the bridge
is washed out. And some-
times it's dark.
And sometimes you lose
your way.

Fun, huh?

When I said,
"My foot is slipping,"
your love, O LORD,
supported me. When
anxiety was great
within me, your con-
solation brought joy to
my soul.

Psalm 94:18–19
(NIV)

But you'll arrive safely.

You have an official
escort to make sure
of that.

I know the LORD
is always with me.
I will not be shaken,
for he is right
beside me.

Psalm 16:8
(NLT)

You don't even
have to drive.

Always live
in confident depend-
ence on
your God.

Hosea 12:6
(NLT)

All the while, keep makin'
your party plans.

So we don't look at the troubles we can see right now; rather, we look forward to what we have not yet seen. For the troubles we see will soon be over, but the joys to come will last forever.

2 Corinthians 4:18
(NLT)

He's saving the best seat
in the house for you.

(Just to make sure you
feel welcome.)

"I will invite everyone who is victorious to sit with me on my throne."

Revelation 3:21
(NLT)

All of heaven is poppin'
the cork and throwing con-
fetti at the thought
of your arrival.

Rejoice and be glad,
because you have a
great reward waiting
for you in heaven.

Matthew 5:12
(NCV)

Feel free to invite a friend—there'll be plenty of room.

I tell you there
is more joy in heaven
over one sinner who
changes his heart and
life, than over
ninety-nine good peo-
ple who don't
need to change.

Luke 15:7
(NCV)

See you there.

His unchanging plan
has always been to
adopt us into his own
family by bringing us
to himself through
Jesus Christ.
And this gave him
great pleasure.

Ephesians 1:5
(NLT)

Oh—and bring your danc-
ing shoes.

"He is a mighty savior. He will rejoice over you with great gladness. With his love, he will calm all your fears. He will exult over you by singing a happy song."

Zephaniah 3:17
(NLT)

My Own Pearls of Wisdom

My Own Pearls of Wisdom

My Own Pearls of Wisdom

My Own Pearls of Wisdom

My Own Pearls of Wisdom

My Own Pearls of Wisdom

My Own Pearls of Wisdom

My Own Pearls of Wisdom

My Own Pearls of Wisdom

My Own Pearls of Wisdom

My Own Pearls of Wisdom

My Own Pearls of Wisdom